Make Success Mandatory

Discovering Your Gift & Giving It Back To The World

Make Success Mandatory

*Discovering Your Gift & Giving It Back
To The World*

Jeremy Scott

Make Success Mandatory

Discovering Your Gift & Giving It Back To the World

Author: Jeremy Scott

All rights reserved. No part of this publication may be reproduced or transmitted in any form or by any means, electronic or mechanical, including photocopy, recording, or any information storage and retrieval system, without the prior written permission of the writer & publisher Jeremy Scott. Except in the case of reviewers who wish to write a review and quote short passages for newspapers, magazines or other platforms, these cases require written approval from Jeremy Scott. To contact please email: jeremyscottfitness@hotmail.com

© Copyright Jeremy Scott, 2014. All rights reserved.

ISBN: 13: 978-1500593711 (CreateSpace Assigned)

Jeremy Scott: Jeremy Scott Fitness LLC

jeremyscottfitness@hotmail.com

Table of Contents

Acknowledgements 5
About This Book 7
Introduction: Master of Failure 9
Exercise #1: Do you sincerely want the most from your Life? 13
Exercise #2: Understanding the gift of 86,400 that make up your 30,000 15
Exercise #3: Attitude is Everything 17
Exercise #4: Stop Worrying & Wishing 19
Exercise #5: Decisions Determination Destiny 21
Exercise #6: What you decide today will shape the rest of your Life 23
Exercise #7: Find yourself: Be yourself 25
Exercise #8: Knowing What Matters Most to You 27
Exercise #9: It's going to be Hard: Life is Hard: Embrace it ... 29
Exercise #10: Stop caring what others think of your Journey 35
Exercise #11: Just Be Nice to people 37
Exercise #12: Be Obsessed with a Purpose 39
Exercise #13: Get Happy, Be Happy, Stay Happy 41
Exercise #14: Forgive & Move Forward 43
Exercise #15: Self-Acceptance: Love Your Body: Love Your Life 45
Exercise #16: Fighting for your Future 47

Exercise #17: Don't make it about the Money 49

Exercise #18: Write it down: Make a list check it twice 53

Exercise #19: Perfect Preparation 57

Exercise #20: Know your "Shoulds" vs your "Musts" 59

Exercise #21: Finally, Making Success Mandatory 61

Exercise #22: The 7 Day Mandatory Mindset Assessment 63

My hopes for your NEW successful Life 67

About The Author 69

Acknowledgements

I would like to acknowledge and thank the following people: All the amazing individuals I have had the opportunity to coach in Arizona & online over the past 5 years at Jeremy Scott Fitness. Without meeting and working with all of you this book wouldn't have come to life.

To my partner in crime, my fiancé Heather Schroeder thanks for putting up with my obsessive behavior and supporting all my visions from day one. Special thanks to the amazing editing skills of Monica Millage & Susie Hardt, I am forever grateful for your help with this project.

To all of you who have believed in me even when I didn't really believe in myself I am thankful for the role you have played; it starts with my personal assistant Janet Navarre; my old man Perry Scott, Dave Navarre, Kelly Groff, Jeremy Belter, Ben Novak, Dave Dreas, Kim Maes, Brett & Inga Darrow, B.J. Letcher, Kelly Olexa & FitFluential, Padraig O'Brien, my old coach & English teacher Mike Costello, Damon Moschetto & everyone at the FCG, the good folks at MRI/PROLAB & Reebok; the entire KV Family; and all my real lifelong friends like Connor Stoltz you have all played a significant role in this process and more importantly in my life.

They say we are the average of the five people we associate with the most, so I thank you all again for associating with me, constantly lifting me up and always supporting me.

About This Book

Thank you for investing your time into this book, as you will learn your time is the most valuable thing you can give to anything or anyone; so again I sincerely thank you for investing your time with me.

This book is NOT just about making success mandatory.

This book is about making a better life not just for yourself but also for everyone around you, that's what real success is, giving back to the world.

This book is about not being afraid to fail, and venturing outside your comfort zone.

This book is about looking within, questioning yourself, finding out who you really are and what your life is truly about.

This book is meant to be interactive; it's meant to get your mind working and your blood flowing. I want you to ignite your inner go-getter and have you jumping from one epic thought, goal, and inspiration to the next.

My hope and intention is for all of you to find an idea, a dream, and a vision of what you want most out of your time. I want you to discover your path, your passion, your love, your why, your gift and your calling in life.

You are all here for a greater purpose, you all matter, you all have unique, special amazing gifts that only you can offer the world and I want to uncover those with you.

From here on out, please promise me you will stop wasting your talents, your gifts, your ideas, your dreams, and most importantly your time. You owe it to yourself and to those around you to give nothing less than your best each day.

"To give anything less than your best, is to sacrifice the gift."

– Steve Prefontaine

Sincerely, thank you again for investing your time with me.

Introduction: Master of Failure

> "I've missed more than 9000 shots in my career. I've lost almost 300 games. 26 times, I've been trusted to take the game winning shot and missed. I've failed over and over and over again in my life. And that is why I succeed."
>
> – Michael Jordan

I, Jeremy Scott, am a self-proclaimed "master of failure." Probably not the best way to start a book on making success mandatory in your life, talking about how I have personally failed over and over in my life. Or maybe it's exactly the right way to start things off?

I failed at just about everything I have attempted in my life.

The first time I took the ACT in high school I received a 17. It took me three more attempts to squeeze out a college worthy 26.

During my high school and collegiate basketball career I never won a single conference, regional, state or national championship. It's not what one would consider a winning career.

My college math placement exam put me into the lowest level math course offered. I failed numerous exams and had to attend tutoring on a nightly basis. I would meet the professor every single week early in the morning during his office hours for extra help just to pull out a "C" grade for the term.

Through hard work, a fear of failing, and what I like to call "grinding it out", I managed to earn my undergraduate degree with Cum Laude honors. My 1st year post-college living in the "real world" I went on over 50 interviews, being rejected an impressive 45 out of 50 times.

The jobs I did get, I often quit within a few months before they could fire me. I wasn't producing, making progress, contributing or creating much value to the companies that did hire me. Mix in a few failed attempts to take jobs in different states; thinking a change of city or state would help me "un-suck", to cut a long story short, it didn't.

No matter the environment I still lacked passion, remained unmotivated, became slightly depressed, and was the farthest thing from a success.

These are just a few things I am now comfortable talking about; they really don't even scratch the surface of my "personal life" failures.

I was on the road to average, 24 years old living at home with my "Old Man" searching for answers. There was a point that I lost confidence in myself, after several failures, some serious medical and personal issues I was at my rock bottom personally.

After a few rough months, I received a random intoxicated 3:00 a.m. voicemail from my good friend Ryan Peterson in Phoenix, AZ asking me to come live with him. At first I didn't think much of it as my life was in Minnesota, why would I move all the way out to Arizona?

But then I got to really thinking, I started asking myself the tough questions.

What life was I really living?

What did I have to look forward to?

What was the worst thing that could happen if I moved?

After days of talking to myself I looked in the mirror and said, "Jeremy, if you are waiting for a sign, this is it." I figured if I failed at this adventure I could always move back in with my Old Man and take back my average, sad, depressing life. So why not move out to AZ?

In that moment I decided to take massive action. I packed up my car with my life savings of $2,500, zero connections, no plan, no interviews set up and headed out to a city and a state I had never visited. At the time it just seemed like another move for me. Little did I know, that phone call, that decision, and that move would alter my entire life forever.

> **"There is no such thing as success without failure."**
>
> – Melissa Ohnoutka

Anyone who says they haven't failed miserably at something is either lying to you or just coasting through life not even remotely scratching the surface of their potential to know what they are capable of.

Failure is a real, genuine, authentic thing that happens along the way to success, it's the greatest motivator and educator for many of us. I know it has been for me.

It has come to be my belief, my truth, and my religion; that all my failures up to this point, of which there are many, have been the foundation of any successes I have had. Without these failures or now "life lessons" as I call them, I would have no true success in my life.

Exercise #1: Do you sincerely want the most from your Life?

Ray Lewis once said something that stuck with me from the second I heard it...

"I am pissed off for greatness, because if you ain't pissed off for greatness that means you're OK with being mediocre."

So I ask you...

Are you pissed off for greatness?

Think about it for a few seconds, are you pissed off to reach greatness in your life?

If the answer is NO, you might as well throw this book in the trash and go on living your average mediocre life.

If you are still reading, I assume you are NOT okay with being mediocre and you are pissed off to be great in every arena of your life.

What I am about to share with you are simply my rules, views, and thoughts on how to make the most of not only your life but also the lives of others around you.

I measure success not by trophies, accolades or financial gains. To me, the start of being successful comes from living life on your own terms, your own rules, doing what you want, when you want, and doing things exactly how you want.

The biggest key however lies in not only what you can do for yourself, but also what you can do for others. Changing, improving, teaching and inspiring others to live a better & happier life, that is absolute success in my eyes.

So let's start off with some simple questions...

Are you living your life on your own terms?

Do you run your day or does your day run you?

Are you writing the story of your life, or are you living out someone else's dream?

Are you giving the world your full potential each day?

Is there something more you could be doing with your precious time?

Exercise #2: Understanding the gift of 86,400 that make up your 30,000

What can you do with this time? What will you do with this time?

When the clock strikes midnight you are given a gift of 86,400 seconds to run, play, smile, cry, laugh, work, love, and chase your wildest dreams.

Every second, minute, hour, day, week, month we receive is a precious gift that many of us fail to use and appreciate for what it is. Your time is the most valuable thing you are ever given. We never know how much of it is guaranteed and none of it is promised to us, so it's our duty to make the absolute most of it.

The biggest regret and tragedy for most people is thinking that they will have time to start living the life they envision. Sadly, many of them end up looking back on their life wishing they would have done more with their time.

You will never have more time in your life than you do right now, let me say that again because you need to really understand that concept to fully grasp what this book is saying to you, **"You will never have more time in your life than you do right now."**

So, if inspiration strikes you, grab it, run with it and don't look back!

As we begin I want you to write the next statement down and stick it somewhere you will see it every day when you wake up, as a reminder so you never forget.

This is your life, you are not going to get another one, and there is no such thing as "just another day." Every single day, every 86,400 seconds you get are unique; you and only you are responsible for the quality of those seconds.

So what are you going to do with the next week, month, and year of your life?

You and only you can dictate how awesome, exciting, and badass it can be.

The Blessing of 30,000 Amazing Miracles

On average give or take a few days, 30,000 is the number of days most of us get.

30,000 days to smile, laugh, love, play and enjoy everything the world has to offer.

30,000 opportunities to change, inspire, and impact the lives of others.

To put it into perspective for you, if you are 25 years old you have about 20,000 days left… if you are 55 years old you have about 10,000 days left…

Enjoy each moment, each experience, and each 86,400 as an amazing gift and I ask you to please live it like it's your last because someday it will be.

Exercise #3: Attitude is Everything

Your attitude is everything. We can't control many of the things that happen to us in life but we can always control our attitude towards those things.

I break down attitude into four basic personality types; four different types of people...

Glass Empty–Glass Half Empty–Glass Half Full–Glass Full

You know the types, we have all met them before, the person who is always negative, mad, upset and complains about everything – the "glass empty" person.

On the flipside there are the few who see the world not as an obstacle but as an opportunity, they somehow seem to find the good in all situations - the "glass full" person.

And then there is the middle, half-empty, half full crowd where I think a majority of people fall.

Do you know what type of "glass" you are?

The better question is what type of "glass" person do you want to be?

We all create our own little world by the way we choose to see it through the glass, be it full or empty or somewhere in between. It's this view that creates how our lives turn out, they become empty or they become full based on how we choose to see things.

I challenge you to make the next 7 days amazing...

For the next 7 days you can choose to focus on your opportunity, success, gifts, and everything you **do** have in your life.

Or you can choose to focus on all the roadblocks, fears, worries, regrets and things you **don't** have in your life.

The choice is 100% yours…

What I can promise you is; whatever you focus on you're going to get. If you simply wake up and approach each day with a "glass full" mentality to everything, your entire world will start to change.

Most of your day-to-day problems are not life or death issues, and ultimately are only small roadblocks testing you on your way to success, happiness, and the life you are working towards.

Exercise #4: Stop Worrying & Wishing

Many of you have heard this before...

"Worrying is like a rocking chair, it gives you something to do but it gets you nowhere"

Or my personal favorite...

"You can wish in one hand and shit in another, see which one fills up faster"

It might sound a little harsh but truer words have probably never been spoken.

I bring these up because wishing and worrying does nothing but waste precious time you could be out working for your dreams.

Most problems people worry about never come to materialize. Meaning the process of worrying itself was the issue; the anticipation of the problem was far greater than the problem itself.

What good has worrying ever really done for you?

An easy fix: stop worrying about tomorrow and focus on enjoying today, focus your efforts on kicking ass in everything you do today. Really appreciating every second of this day and this moment. Work in the present; love the "now" while it's here.

You can wish for something or you can work for something, it's that simple. Even people who win the lottery have to get up off their ass and go buy a ticket. They didn't just sit home and wish to win; there was at least a little work involved.

I hear people say it all the time…

"I wish I had more money"

"I wish I was in better shape"

"I wish I had a better job"

The ONLY people who actually end up getting their "wishes" are the ones who go out and actually work for them day after day.

"Good things come to those who wait, but only the things left by those who hustle." – Abraham Lincoln

Moving forward, don't worry about failing, don't worry about what might go wrong, don't worry about anything, just start working towards the things you want & deserve.

Don't worry about it…

Don't wish for it…

Just work for it…

Exercise #5: Decisions Determination Destiny

Success is a result of your decisions & your determination to see those decisions through day after day, which ultimately shapes your destiny.

It's your decisions not your circumstances that shape your destiny

You decide everyday what you do with your time...

You decide whom you spend your time with...

You decide where you spend your money...

You decide to read, learn and educate yourself...

You decide to eat right or not...

You decide to workout or sit on your ass...

If you want to change your life, and really shape your destiny, you need to start deciding how to best spend your time.

Decide what kind of person you want to be.

Decide what you really stand for.

Decide what kind of life you really want.

Decide how you want to be remembered.

Once you have made some of these real life decisions, or what I like to call "gut check" decisions, you must become committed to them. Then begin to create your determination plan.

5 Steps to creating a Determination Plan:

1. Make a decision: Decide what you want.
2. Take massive action.
3. Be determined & stay committed.
4. Decide that there is always a solution.
5. Never stop.

The fastest way to change your life is by making a choice.

By making a REAL choice, by deciding on a new direction, you are saying: "There is no going back to my old life."

This is the new path and I am determined to make it happen.

Make just one decision today decide right now maybe something you have been putting off, maybe something that's been holding you back.

Make the Decision become Determined shape your Destiny

Exercise #6: What you decide today will shape the rest of your Life

Ask Great Questions: Get Great Answers: Create a Great Life

You want a greater life? You need to be asking greater questions...

Seems simple right? Think about it we ask ourselves internal questions all day long.

"Why can't I ever catch a break?"

"Why can't I have that job?"

"Why is life so unfair?"

The questions we ask ourselves and others can easily dictate the immediate quality of our life.

The questions you ask yourself are a guide to your thoughts, your energy, and ultimately your actions. Sometimes having a better more fulfilling life comes from something as simple as asking better, more fulfilling questions.

Think about it, what if you just asked yourself different questions each day?

Instead of asking yourself things like...

Why do bad things always happen to me?

What's wrong with me?

When will I ever catch a break?

Try asking yourself…

What am I grateful for today?

What can I do to make things better?

What can I be happy about right now?

What is one thing I am looking forward to doing?

It's a simple way of changing how you look at the problem, asking a different question in the same situation to get a totally different positive answer.

Quick daily question list I ask myself each morning:

How can I improve the lives of those around me?

How can I remember this day for the rest of my life?

How many people care about me and are depending on me today?

One of the biggest questions I came across was a spin off from the old JFK quote. Once I heard it my mindset immediately switched gears. It went something like this…

"The problem with most people is they are always asking, what can I get from this life? What can this life offer me? When they should really be asking, what can I give back to this life?"

Exercise #7: Find yourself: Be yourself

Do you know who you really are?

If you can't be yourself at your job, with your friends, or your family, you will never truly be happy in your life I can guarantee you that.

You can make millions of dollars, have the greatest job, the most amazing spouse, and the most loving family but if you can't truly be yourself you will be miserable inside because it's all built on a fake you.

I can say this with 100% certainty because this was once my reality. For years I had to be one person in public, at school, at work, and another person in private with my friends, family, and significant other.

Trying to be something or someone you are not is like poison to yourself and everything you do. You will find a great freedom in really being yourself and when you are being yourself, sincere and honest, you are never really wrong, every action just seems to be right.

Take a second for a little self-reflection:

Who are you inside?

What are you passionate about?

What things bring your life joy?

What do you love to talk about?

Whether you are introverted, extroverted, high energy, low energy, maniac crazy, or calm and collected, own your personality to its core.

It's when we can truly be ourselves and only then can we find absolute happiness.

No amount of money, fake love, praise, awards, accolades or promotions can make you truly happy if you are living a lie or pretending to be something you are not.

Eventually it will exhaust you and you will look back on a life that was lived as a lie, and I can't imagine anyone wants to do that.

You have something important, special and very unique to give the world. There is no way for you to give the world that gift if you are busy trying to be someone else or something you're not.

When you finally know, embrace, and become yourself; then and only then can you finally start living your dreams.

This is your life, this is your time, your one chance to make your mark.

So I ask you again: Do you know who you really are?

Exercise #8: Knowing What Matters Most to You

At various stages of your life you will place the majority of your time, your effort, your feelings, and your energy in various areas according to what matters most to you.

Knowing what really matters is crucial to not only your success but also your personal fulfillment and happiness in life.

Think about it...

What matters more: the awards you win, or the person you become?

What matters more: the people in your life or material possessions you buy?

What matters more: your job title or the lives you change?

What matters more: how you spend your money or how you spend your time?

Breakdown your life into sections of what matters most...

Grab a pen and paper and write this down in sections, think pie graph...

Breakdown your priorities of what matters in terms of % - for example you spend 40% of your time on your career, family equates to maybe 30% of your time "etc."

See what truly matters most to you be it family, friends, career, finances, religion, traveling, health, community service. Give them all a % adding up to 100%.

Now look at how your time in terms of % is allotted. Look at the amount of time you really spend on the things that matter and the things that don't.

Are your values of what matters aligned with how you spend a % of your time?

I will say it again every day, every 86,400 you get is a precious valuable gift.

For this reason, it is crucial you know who and what really matters in your life.

If your family is your priority but you are spending all your time working, something needs to change.

Every week take a few minutes to think and ask the very basic question…

What REALLY matters MOST in my life?

Examine if you are really spending your time on what matters most to you, or are you just wasting away the days, weeks, months, and years on things that aren't really that important?

Let what matters most to you guide your life in the right direction.

Exercise #9: It's going to be Hard: Life is Hard: Embrace it

My old man in his old school blue-collar wisdom unknowingly gave me two great pieces of advice growing up. The first was a simple phrase: **"tough shit."**

To put this into better context, this phrase was usually followed by some request or plea I made to my old man for something I wanted but didn't really need; such as money for video games or new shoes. I would ask and his standard reply would be "tough shit." It was simple, to the point and I got the message loud and clear.

The other little gem, which I have shared previously in this book, went like this: **"Jeremy, you can wish in one hand and shit in the other, see which one fills up faster."**

Now my old man might not win any poetry contests, but after years of thinking he was just a "hard-ass" and the world owed me something; I finally got the message.

Indirectly he taught me one of the most important life lessons there is; that Life is HARD and the things you want are going to require hard work.

Now flash-forward to my adult life, I hear this phrase all the time, **"It's too hard."**

Probably the biggest excuse I come across when we really breakdown all the bullshit and excuses people come up with is: "it's just too hard."

Let me give you a few examples, it usually starts with "Jeremy"

It's too hard to go back to school…

It's too hard to find the time to workout…

It's too hard to start my own business…

It's too hard to eat right when I travel…

It's too hard to wake up and train before work…

This list of EXCUSES is endless but you get where I am going with this. The reality is, whatever your perception is will be your truth. Many of these people believe this shit, they have sold themselves on the reality that it's honestly **"too hard"** to do these things and make these simple changes to improve their life.

But the absolute truth is, EVERYTHING WE DO IS HARD!

In my mind you have to choose what HARD you really want and which HARD is going to help you and which one is going to hurt you.

"Nothing worth having comes easy"

If it was easy everyone would do it, it's the "HARD" that makes it amazing.

I admit it's hard working out when you're tired, it's hard eating right day after day without seeing immediate results, it's hard pushing through the bad days…

But you know what else is HARD?

It is also hard to go shopping because your current clothes don't fit and you need to buy bigger sizes.

It is hard to go to a job you hate day after day.

It is hard to feel confident when you feel fat.

It is hard to keep up with your kids when you are exhausted and unhealthy.

Hopefully you can see what I am getting at with these examples.

At the end of the day we all get to pick which hard will be our hard.

I worked a 9-5 job in corporate America, Monday-Friday, sitting in a cubicle, doing some remedial task I didn't care about for average pay and while that might sound easy to some, it was so HARD for me!

It's hard to wake up and go to a job you hate.

It's hard to work when you are uninspired.

For me it was hard to have an "average" job.

For me it was hard to live an "average" life.

So, I went out and changed my HARD.

Life is HARD you guys, no matter if you are chasing your dreams or just going through the motions.

It's supposed to be hard.

The "HARD" is what challenges you, changes you, and makes you a badass.

Almost every great thing you have in this life will take some type of struggle to achieve. You need to go through the pain sometimes to get the prize, but how sweet it is when you finally get what you have worked so hard for.

So the question is: Which HARD do you want?

Do you want to endure the HARD of training and eating right? Or do you want to endure the HARD of being overweight, unhealthy and depressed?

Do you want to endure the HARD of hating your job? Or endure the HARD of chasing your dreams?

Do you want the HARD that sacrifice, dedication, and persistence brings? Or do you want the HARD of regret?

I will tell you from personal experience: DON'T look back on your life in any arena, sports, school, relationships, business or anything in between wishing you would have given more to make it work or be your absolute best.

Looking back on a life filled with regrets; now that's a "HARD" you have to live with for the rest of your life and it's a constant feeling that never really goes away.

The choice of which HARD you want is ultimately up to you and only you!

Like many of you I wasn't given anything in this life. I didn't start out on 3rd base. I had to work my ass off and continue to do so every single day for everything I have and it's HARD. But I know how HARD it can be on the other side too, so I will take this HARD with a smile and keep working!

Now is the time for you to STOP making excuses about how HARD everything is. Accept it, embrace it, and go out and get what you want.

Exercise #10: Stop caring what others think of your Journey

One of the very first steps you take on the road to being a successful bad ass is no longer caring what other people think of you.

Most of my life I was told to just "fit in." I was asked countless times to just "go with the flow" and "be more like the other kids."

The problem was I wasn't like the "other kids," maybe it was my OCD, and maybe it was because I am naturally so introverted. Whatever the reason, I struggled with it for years and years; even to this day there are many things I don't view, understand, or process like most people.

But it wasn't until I literally stopped trying to fit in and just did what felt natural that my life started to change, doors started to open and my happiness increased tenfold.

STOP TRYING TO "FIT IN"

Never be afraid to embrace who you truly are. People will judge you for it, sometimes ridicule you for it but pay them no mind. Their idea of who you are and who you should be means nothing when it's all said and done.

At the end of the day when you look in the mirror you know in your heart of hearts you are being true to yourself and that will bring you a sense of self most can only imagine grasping.

The further away I got from the "norm": the 9-5 office pool, working for the weekend's lifestyle, the more I realized it was all a bullshit fictional prison people accept as a "way of life."

You can do, be, go, and achieve just about anything you put your mind to if YOU think outside the box and just be who YOU really are 24-7-365.

Steve Jobs said it better than I ever could:

"Here's to the crazy ones. The misfits. The rebels. The troublemakers. The round pegs in the square holes. The ones who see things differently.

They're not fond of rules. And they have no respect for the status quo. You can quote them, disagree with them, glorify or vilify them. About the only thing you can't do is ignore them.

Because they change things. They push the human race forward. And while some may see them as the crazy ones, we see genius. Because the people who are crazy enough to think they can change the world, are the ones who do."

Don't let what you're "supposed" to do replace what you truly want to do.

Exercise #11: Just Be Nice to people

This might be the most underrated and most important lesson people can learn in life simply being nice to people.

If you are a sincere, genuine, nice person you will be successful in everything and I mean everything you do in life.

How does one start to be nice?

Seems easy enough but for a long time people thought I was an asshole and some people still might think that. Being ultra quiet, reserved, shy and having a larger muscular build people would often assume I was this arrogant, self-centered asshole.

It's not that I was an asshole, it's just I didn't really know how to convey who I was and how "nice" I was inside. Refer back to exercise #7 in this book about knowing who you are when dealing with these judgmental types.

Now, with that said it's no fun having everyone think you're an asshole when you really are just a nice normal dude trying to enjoy life.

So, here are a few steps I have learned along the way that have helped me and they might just help you convey your inner awesome and show people how nice you really are.

Step 1: SMILE – seems simple enough but for years I hated my smile and never did it, so automatically I was seen as a hard-cold-uninviting person. My advice: smile more, smile all the time, smile to strangers, and smile when you meet people, it makes all the difference in the world not only for you but also to others around you.

Just smiling at someone can have a huge impact on his or her day, maybe even change his or her mood from bad to great – you have that immense power in a simple smile. So smile big and smile often.

Step 2: Listen 1st–Talk 2nd –most people don't listen enough, they simply wait for their turn to talk. We all know these types of people. It's annoying to talk to them, so please don't be one of them.

The world needs more listeners – really hear what the other person is saying. Process their comments, give great feedback, be engaged, be genuine, and be honest. If you can do that all your daily interactions will be much more powerful and meaningful.

Step 3: Be Positive– negativity is a contagious cancer that spreads through locker rooms, offices, households, and everywhere you bring it. Be the positive force, be the bright light, and be the example everywhere you go. It's just as contagious.

The average person can't stand negative people and negativity. They don't want to hear about your issues, odds are they have plenty of their own problems to deal with. I heard the great coach Lou Holtz once say…

"Never tell your problems to anyone…20% don't care and the other 80% are glad you have them."

Immediately after hearing this it made me stop and think about how I sounded complaining and whining to my friends and family about my issues. Instead of dumping my problems on the world, I always strive to be the "glass all full" person, I suggest you try and do the same. Not only will you enrich and enjoy your own life more, but you will also help lift up everyone you encounter in the process.

Exercise #12: Be Obsessed with a Purpose

This falls in line with finding your passion; to me being passionate and obsessed bleeds over into one another. For those of you who really know me, know that I have some of the worst OCD there is. The things that go on in my head the patterns, repetitive habits, and tendencies are sickening.

But I have managed to channel my obsessive compulsiveness into my passion and it's this obsession that allows me to excel in any area of my life once I become fixated with it.

When you find your true passion for what you love it becomes an obsession.

Finding something that you love, something that keeps you up at night, something you can't stop talking or thinking about; those are generally great places to start when searching for what you are truly passionate about.

The biggest reason I became involved in coaching and training wasn't just for the fitness aspect, it wasn't just for the nutrition aspect, but rather the guidance of helping and coaching people to find success through changing their mindset. I guess I always wanted to be an educator, someone who helps others. The health industry just happened to be a great audience and "classroom" for me to start in.

Do it for your Heart & Soul NOT for the Money

I say it all the time: "most of this stuff I would do for free because I love it" and it's true. I would write blogs, articles, and books and make videos even if nobody ever read or watched them. Why, you ask? Because I feel that's what I am born to do. I feel my gift is showing people the only limits they have are the ones they self-impose on themselves; it's my passion, my obsession to help others see their full potential.

If you are going to truly be successful you can't make it just about the money, nobody and I mean nobody's passion is collecting old dirty paper with dead presidents on it. Your passion has to come from within, it has to be authentic or it will die long before you ever reach your goals or make an impact on the world.

Success in anything is hard so you have to love it to your core; you have to have an obsessive passion for it. Because at times it will be so hard you will want to quit. There might even be multiple times you want to give up. However, if you love something sincerely, deeply and truly you will never quit, you will never stop working to make it happen.

Think about it for a second – what do you love in this world?

Do you love your life? Do you love your parents? Do you love your kids?

Now I ask you the question –Would you ever just quit on them?

Exercise #13: Get Happy, Be Happy, Stay Happy

"Happiness only real when shared." –Christopher McCandless

Happiness, like most things in life is a choice; sometimes we get jaded and lost in the small bullshit problems of life that we fail to see the big picture stuff.

I live in Scottsdale, AZ in my opinion the greatest city in America. The weather is as beautiful as the people and the restaurants, sports, nightlife, and shopping are all amazing.

However, sometimes living in a place like this people forget how good they truly have it. We get spoiled; we forget so many people in the world have it much, much worse than we do. Most of our problems are laughable when you think big picture.

Many people have forgotten how to get happy, be happy and stay happy…

It reminds me of this quote I read a few years ago…

"If you have food in your fridge, clothes on your back, a roof over your head and a place to sleep you are richer than 74% of the world.

If you have money in the bank, your wallet, and some spare change you are among the top 8% of the worlds wealthy.

If you woke up this morning with more health than illness you are more blessed than the million people who will not survive this week.

If you have never experienced the danger of battle, the agony of imprisonment or torture, or the horrible pangs of starvation you are luckier than 500 million people alive and suffering.

If you can read this message you are more fortunate than 3 billion people in the world who cannot read it at all."

Sometimes when I start thinking about my "problems" or how "unhappy" I am, I simply pull this quote out and within a few seconds I come back to reality.

Take a good look at your life, your family, your friends, and all the people who matter to you and all the people you matter to. If you really dig down deep into your life of what really makes you happy – you will see you have been happy all along; sometimes we just need a reminder of how truly badass our life really is.

"Remember that happiness is a way to travel, not a destination." Roy Goodman

Exercise #14: Forgive & Move Forward

I am not just talking about forgiving others here.

I am talking about forgiving yourself.

"The weak can never forgive. Forgiveness is the attribute of the strong." Gandhi

Most of you have had people do you wrong more times than you can count in your life; people lie, cheat, steal, wound and hurt us from birth…it's part of life.

But so is forgiveness… When you can learn to forgive someone who has done you wrong in your life, you aren't just doing it for him or her in all reality you are doing it for you.

Forgiving people does something to us. When we can let go, it sets us free to move forward and live life free from the pain and struggle we were once living with.

Admittedly, forgiveness is something I have struggled with most of my life. I held onto grudges, hate, and resentment for many people for many years. What good did it do me? None, resenting others never benefited my life in any way shape or form.

The #1 thing I found out – not forgiving is a poison to your heart and soul.

I thought I could use that hate, all that resentment as motivation, as fuel to get what I wanted, but I found out after many years you can't build something positive & great on negativity and contempt.

When I finally learned to let go and forgive those who had wronged me in the past, my life started to change quickly. I was finally able to start living at peace with myself and who I was, which allowed me to contribute, give back, and start helping others with this internal positivity.

"The truth is, unless you let go, unless you forgive yourself, unless you forgive the situation, unless you realize that the situation is over, you cannot move forward." – Steve Maraboli

My advice – just let it all go – life is too short to be living in the rearview. There are far better things ahead for you in this life than anything you are holding onto – so leave them behind. The world needs you to be here in the right state of mind so forgive and get moving forward.

> **"Throughout life people will make you mad, disrespect you and treat you bad. Let God deal with the things they do, because hate in your heart will consume you too." – Will Smith**

Exercise #15: Self-Acceptance: Love Your Body: Love Your Life

External acceptance of your body leads to internal happiness & health

You need to accept your body, love it, cherish it and treat it like the only place you have to live…oh wait, it is the only place you have to live.

For better or worse the body you are living in is yours and it's yours for life. Accept your flaws, all of them, as they are uniquely yours to own.

Remember you are a real person with flaws –not a walking magazine cover!

Now to some degree I think we all feel "self-conscious" of certain areas of our body be it breasts, stomach, arms, legs, butt, whatever it is most of us have something we don't love about our bodies.

I think that's a normal feeling, we can all work on some things we don't like…but when it becomes an obsession – taking up hours of your day thinking about it, staring in the mirror at your "trouble spots" day after day, not wearing or ALWAYS wearing certain clothes to hide your "flaws" it becomes more of an unhealthy habit or disorder.

I am here to tell you guys – we are all a little crazy, but listen when I say "LOVE WHAT YOU HAVE, LOVE WHAT YOU WERE GIVEN and WORK HEALTHILY, SAFELY, and POSITIVELY TO CHANGE the things you don't love just yet!"

The society we live in, the culture of certain fitness circles, comparisons to models, actors, actresses, and images we see on TV and magazines all create a false sense of what we are supposed to look like.

Women you have it the worst... this Photoshop, airbrushed, bullshit they feed you ladies isn't real...it's not even remotely realistic and even if it was real, that girl on the magazine cover probably has 2-3 things she is working on that she doesn't like about herself as well.

How do I know? Because I was one of those people. I have been on magazine covers, billboards, and television and hated my own image for a long time.

If you take anything away from this exercise let it be "NEVER and I mean NEVER compare yourself to anyone else. Your genetics, your goals, your stresses, your body is 100% yours DON'T be concerned with every imperfection it's those imperfections that make us unique, make us special and make us sexy!

Start loving your body and shortly after you will start truly loving your life.

Exercise #16: Fighting for your Future

I know, I know, I am "Mr. 86,400" making the most of the moment, mastering today, living my life in a 24-hour window however...

We all need a purpose, a passion, and an obsession to dominate our future.

A bright, inspiring, compelling, and "PULLING" future makes it easy to get up, go out, and get after it every day.

Having a DREAM – having a future – gives you some meaning to move forward...

So, Step #1 would be DREAM and DREAM BIG, have a compelling vision that pulls you to the future.

The reasons I say have a dream, goal or vision to "PULL" you through is simple, when life gets tough, when things get hard, when you get punched in your face it gets hard to push yourself.

We talk a lot about pushing yourself to do more, and that's easy when everything is going right, but when times get tough it's much harder to give yourself that massive push to get things done.

But, if you have something pulling you forward into the future this journey becomes much easier to keep fighting, and to keep moving forward.

Pushing yourself can get you started on your goals, dreams, and plans for the future. But it's that "PULLING," that compelling constant pull that will ultimately get you through.

Quick steps to getting started…

1. Find the DREAM: make it a focused vision; see yourself doing it a year from now.

2. Dreams have NO LIMITS – think BIG here – almost nothing is impossible.

3. What would you try today if you knew there was zero chance of failure?

4. Outline a detailed list – specific "musts" to get started on this dream.

5. Visualize it – see it in your mind – really see it happen in your thoughts before it ever comes to life – everything great happens in your mind before it does in real life.

6. Write down WHY you need to do this and write down WHY you will do it.

7. Do something every single day to move one step closer to this DREAM.

"So many of our dreams at first seem impossible, then seem improbable, and then when we summon the will, they soon seem inevitable. – Christopher Reeve

Exercise #17: Don't make it about the Money

"Money is numbers and numbers never end. If it takes money to be happy, your search for happiness will never end." - Bob Marley

I touched on this already, but I think we need to get clear about where money fits in on the success ladder. Life can't just be about the money. I will say this again your childhood dreams did not revolve around paper with the photos of dead presidents on it.

They say, "Money can't buy happiness" well that's not 100% true. For some people, money can in fact buy happiness. People love material things a new house, new car, new jewelry, staying in the nicest resorts, eating at the finest restaurants. I know many people whose money does buy them a form of happiness. Personally speaking from being dead broke to where I am today; having money can make your life easier and happier. But it's only momentary happiness. New things get old, shiny toys become worn out, and the happiness starts to fade.

The saying should be "money can't buy absolute happiness"

You can have all the money in the world, buy everything your heart desires but if you aren't progressing as a person emotionally, spiritually, if you have nobody to share your ideas, thoughts, feelings and time with your happiness will never be absolute.

Money for most of us is a necessary evil to get by in the society we have created, and we all want more of it, because money allows us to do and buy some pretty badass stuff. It only becomes a problem when our pursuit of it blinds us and steals away our time from what really matters in our life.

How Much Money Do YOU Need To Be Happy?

You and only you can answer that.

I don't have all the answers but I can tell you from personal experience, I make more money today as I type this than I ever have in my life. More money than I ever even imagined was possible for a guy like me.

What I can tell you in all honesty is this; money does make your life easier if you let it. But what money doesn't do is motivate me to do more, be better, and it sure as hell doesn't wake me up at 4am excited to go to work...

Money can't do that, it doesn't have the power to, and it doesn't matter that much to me. It's just paper or numbers in an account at the end of the day.

You know what does get me up at 4am every day?

Helping people, connecting, writing, inspiring, educating and changing lives does that. The money that comes along with all those things is just a nice benefit.

In all reality, I would do 99% of this stuff for FREE if I could, but that's not the world today. We all need to have money to feel safe, secure, pay bills, and take care of our families.

I like to compare my career and the money I make to training and working out.

I workout because I love it, it's who I am; the by-product just happens to be I get to feel and look amazing because of it.

The money you make is the same way, find your passion, love what you do and you will make more money than you ever dreamed of. At least that's been my experience.

Our lives are miracles and sometimes we forget that. This adventure we call life is amazing but it's short, so short, and focusing most of your time just chasing paper is a mistake I promise you that.

One last piece of moneymaking advice:

All this money you make, you can't take it with you when you're gone, and I know your family and friends would much rather spend time with you while you are here than spend your money when you're six feet deep.

Don't lose focus on what matters most today. Tell the ones you care about you love them, spend time with them, do what makes you happy, touch as many lives and help as many people as possible, and the money part will work itself out.

"Never go into business purely to make money. If that's the motive you are better off doing nothing." – Richard Branson

Exercise #18: Write it down: Make a list check it twice

So simple, so easy, so effective yet often neglected by millions of people every day trying to chase and reach their goals…

Face the Facts – Writing It Down Makes a Difference

"Dr. Gail Matthews, a psych professor at Dominican University in California, conducted a study on goal setting with 267 participants. She found that people are 42% more likely to achieve their goals just by writing them down."

I have found this personally to be true as well. In my professional mastermind group we often talk about writing it down and scheduling any and everything that is important.

If working out is important to you; you must schedule it.

If you have a business meeting that's important you schedule it.

Dentist, Doctor, Massage appointments. You schedule all those things.

You see where I am going with this? If something is important to you, writing it down, scheduling it, and sticking to the schedule ensures you get it done. Your goals are far more important than any small tasks you write down and schedule every day, so why are you not writing down and putting deadlines on your big important goals?

The average person, which you are not since you are still reading this far into the book, will go through life with no real direction or purpose. They wonder through the day wishing and hoping things workout and just magically get done.

The real key is not only writing things down, that's just the start. The real way to ensure you get where you want to go is by being clear, focused and committed to the goals and lists you write down.

"To-Do" List or a "Do-It" List?

Most of you guys are familiar with your "to-do" list. All the things you are supposed to do, plan to do, or need to do for the day, week, month and so on.

Well, I like to take it one step further here and change the game a little bit from "to-do" list to "DO-IT" list.

Sometimes the smallest change even in the language we use when approaching tasks makes the world of difference.

I will touch on "shoulds" vs. "musts" in a later exercise but essentially we are making our list from stuff we should do, to stuff we must do. Let me show you an example below of one of my recent "DO-IT" lists…

DO-IT Items

Learn something new **do-it**

Get an amazing workout in **do-it**

Make someone smile **do-it**

Appreciate all the things I'm happy about **do-it**

Be nice to everyone I encounter **do-it**

Finish the next exercise in my book **do-it**

Tell at least one person I love them **do-it**

Think of how exciting the future is **do-it**

Read something inspiring **do-it**

Now understand these can be things that are BIG goals or small goals –they can be daily, weekly, monthly, even yearly things that you are 100% committed and focused on doing.

My ritual has been to look at this list every morning and every night and see how many of the "DO-IT" items I got done for the day. If for some reason it didn't happen, I jump into a little self-reflection and ask WHY?

With that being said, having checkpoints with dates on them helps me stay on track and see how much closer I am getting each day to the BIGGER goals on my list.

Sometimes just seeing the words written down makes it real. It's a great reality check and sometimes a kick in the ass we need to live up to our full potential.

It also allows us to celebrate and stay motivated when we accomplish a new DO-IT item. Often times the day-to-day things we complete get lost in the shuffle. Reminding yourself of a job well done is sometimes just the recipe to keep pushing for the future.

From here on out create your "DO-IT" list. Everything you "must" get done, everything that is important to you and your life. Every time you complete a "DO-IT" task celebrate it, acknowledge the job is done and appreciate you are one step closer to your dream.

Sounds strange to some, but the small daily rituals, and all the small daily victories ultimately pave the direction your life is headed.

"If you have a goal write it down. If you don't write it down, you don't have a goal –you have a wish." Steve Maraboli

Exercise #19: Perfect Preparation

The old saying goes something like "practice makes perfect" and I always hated hearing that for the simple fact that if you practice like crap how could you make perfect? You can't. Plain and simple if you practice and don't give your all, don't take it serious, don't try to push and improve yourself it will NEVER be perfect.

Perfect Practice & Perfect Preparation Makes Perfect.

Much of our life is spent preparing for the future and that preparation done correctly and consistently is the foundation for success. Think back to your days in Kindergarten. The whole purpose was to prepare you for the 1st grade. 1st grade was to prepare you for the 2nd grade and so on.

The point is preparation is important; it must be done right. If it's not, you will never get to where you ultimately wish to go. There is a reason you can't go from 3rd grade to 9th grade overnight, the same reason you can't go from mailroom clerk to C.E.O. overnight; you are simply not prepared yet.

For this reason you must prepare for success every day.

Prepare to have a great day.

Prepare by reading the right books.

Prepare by making the right friends.

Prepare by asking the right questions.

Prepare by demanding the most from your talents.

Prepare yourself for the challenges and opportunities coming your way.

Success does not come to those who are unprepared; it simply passes those people by because success would only be wasted on those people who failed to be prepared. Success comes to those who are ready, those who are prepared.

Early in my life when things didn't go my way and opportunities were given to others around me I would say things like; "Why didn't I get that offer?" "Why didn't I get that break?" "Why didn't I get that chance?" I always thought it was because I was "unlucky" but it wasn't until I got older I realized there is no such thing as luck. I was simply unprepared to make the most of the opportunities around me; it would have been wasted on me because I was not ready.

If you want success you must be prepared every single day, because it's that preparedness that will inevitably make the difference between you achieving your dreams and missing them. Some opportunities only come once, don't miss them because you weren't ready!

"Luck is what happens when preparation meets opportunity"
– Seneca

Exercise #20: Know your "Shoulds" vs your "Musts"

I heard Tony Robbins talk about raising your standards a few years back and he said one thing that always stuck with me, he broke down "shoulds" vs. "musts."

It's a very basic concept… think in terms of excuses vs. results if that makes it easier.

For the purpose of this exercise a "should" is something you should be doing and might do sometimes but not all the time. Some examples I hear most often include…

"I should start working out"

"I should start eating right"

"I should start writing my own book"

"I should start saving more money"

Now on the other hand a "must" is something you must do, it's something you always do; it becomes a 100% without a doubt "must" in your life. Some examples of these for many of you would be…

"I must brush my teeth every morning"

"I must take a shower each day"

"I must comb my hair before I go to work"

"I must drink water everyday"

Now you can see a "must" is a concrete ritual that you will do, it's a promise you made to yourself to get it done, it's just part of who you are.

Some people's "musts" are to workout every day, eat a healthy diet, and provide enough money to support their family. For other people those things are just "shoulds" in their lives.

It reminds me of the saying...

"If it's important to you, you will find a way. If not you'll find an excuse."

That pretty much sums it up, if you simply look at your life and all the areas you wish to change or improve find the ones you have as "shoulds" or "musts."

Make a list of all those areas you want to change. Don't you think your life would change immediately and drastically for the better by changing your current "shoulds" to "musts"?

Instead of saying to yourself "I should" do something, start saying to yourself "I must" do something and watch your life change, grow, improve and prosper overnight.

Exercise #21: Finally, Making Success Mandatory

Making Success Mandatory in your life is done by making a choice, just deciding that this is your life and this is how things are going to be.

You must have a clear and focused reason for why you are trying to do whatever it is you wish to do.

We talked about this before; you "MUST" have a "WHY." Something that is so compelling, it keeps you going when times get tough.

You need to have enough reasons to see it through, enough reasons to keep going when most people would quit. The reasons and the why must pull you through.

Your Daily Rituals Become Your Reality.

Success & failure are separated by nothing more than consistently following one set of daily rituals compared to another. Following a higher standard of rituals will yield you a higher standard of results.

It's not enough to just use your 86,400 seconds wisely each day. You need to have a clear vision and laser focus to turn your dreams into your reality.

As you prepare to embark on your calling and pursue your passion, follow the steps of those who have tasted success and reached their goals.

All of the successful people I have had the chance to hear speak, meet with, talk with and work with knew the following...

They all knew exactly what they wanted

They all knew exactly why they wanted it

The all knew exactly how they were going to make it happen

They all made sure that every action had an important purpose

"Long ago. I realized that success leaves clues. And that people who produced outstanding results do specific things to create those results." – Tony Robbins

Tony makes a great point. Success does leave clues and so does failure. So make sure you are clear in your vision, and follow the path of those who have paved it for you the right way.

"Success does leave clues, but it doesn't matter if you don't follow them"

Exercise #22: The 7 Day Mandatory Mindset Assessment

My hope at this point is to have said something that sparked your mind to maybe see things in a different light, maybe think about your goals and your life a little differently.

I have created a very simple and effective assessment for you to participate in over the next 7 days. My only request is that you give your absolute best effort and be 100% honest with yourself when asking and answering these questions.

Your success and your failures are 100% the result of your efforts and your actions.

Let's take massive focused action over the next 7 days with this assessment.

Ready-Set-Go Make Success Mandatory...

Step 1 – For the next 7 days focus on ONLY solutions and opportunities not problems. Ask yourself the question; is this really a life altering problem, or simply an opportunity for me to take another step towards being the person I want to be? This covers everything from health, eating, training, and business, personal, you name it. For the next 7 days all you see are opportunities and solutions there are no problems.

Step 2 - For the next 7 days change two things that are currently "shoulds" in your life to "musts." These can be BIG items or small items, but find two things. Maybe it's working out daily, or eating your veggies each day, taking a class, writing a page a night in your book, something that you know you "must" do and take action towards it daily.

Step 3 - For the next 7 days when you wake up, ask and answer the following before you start your day: How can I improve the lives of those around me? How can I remember this day for the rest of my life? The goal is to touch the lives of others around you at least one person per day make it your goal to "make their day" and also do something memorable, exciting, and fun for yourself – who knows, maybe you can even combine the two?

Step 4 – For the next 7 days before you go to bed reflect for a few minutes on everything you are looking forward to. Think about how bright your future is, think about your goals and dreams and how exciting it will be to achieve them. Visually see them in your mind for a few minutes. On the same note sit and reflect what you are currently thankful for. Think about how blessed you are to be living, breathing, and loving your life with those people around you.

Step 5 – For the next 7 days reconnect with family and friends. Write down a short list of 7 people who are important to you; one person for each day of the week and make it your goal to reach out via phone or in person. Many times in our pursuit of making a living we forget to make a life. The result of this pursuit is often times our friends and family get put on hold. Block off just 15 minutes each day to call them or stop and chat with them to reconnect with each other. It just might have a greater impact on the big picture of your success than you think.

The goal is to help you create some new exciting habits and rituals in your life. By taking part in this simple 7-day assessment you are creating some new standards and changing some important "shoulds" to "musts" as well. Having that "Mandatory Mindset" will only help you grow, appreciate, and love your life more and more with each passing day.

After all, as we have learned here, the secret to success lies not only in your own individual happiness but also in the happiness you create for others.

My hopes for your NEW successful Life

Thank you once again for reading this book. I poured my heart and time into it.

I hope it got you thinking, planning, and believing bigger and brighter than you ever have before.

I hope you attack every single "opportunity" with the mindset to make success mandatory in your life.

I hope you know how much you matter and how important you are to the world.

I hope you can see how much potential and how much greatness is inside you.

I hope you realize that success is self-generated and you control your destiny.

I hope you understand how blessed you truly are.

I hope you take away that your life is meant to be a shared experience.

I hope you go on to do amazing things and live an amazing life.

I hope you sincerely understand your success is connected to the amount of happiness you create in the lives of others.

Finally, I hope you discover your gift and give it back to the world; we will all be anxiously waiting for you!

Until next time, eat well, train hard, be nice to people & make success mandatory.

"Life's most persistent and urgent question is, what are you doing for others?"

-Martin Luther King Jr.

About The Author

Jeremy Scott was born and raised in Winona, MN. He attended Waldorf College in Forest City, Iowa on a basketball scholarship and graduated with Cum Laude honors. Upon graduating Jeremy moved across the country numerous times, failing to find a career path and also failing to find his calling, his gift, and fulfillment in his life. The self-proclaimed "master of failure" just couldn't find success in the post-college "real world."

Struggling for a few years to find his way in the world, an abrupt opportunity came his way in the form of a phone call from a friend. Within a few days he had packed up his car with little money and began to drive across the country from wintery Minnesota to rent a spare room at a friend's house in sunny Phoenix, AZ.

Little did he realize this was the monumental decision & a move that would kick start a new chapter in his life. After several unsuccessful interviews and another brief failed attempt in the corporate world. Jeremy ventured out on his own to pursue his passion of helping others by creating Jeremy Scott Fitness in Scottsdale, AZ.

Since the inception of Jeremy Scott Fitness; Jeremy has been able to educate, coach, motivate, and change the lives of thousands of people not only in Arizona but also around the world via his online success coaching programs.

In addition to running his own company, Jeremy also co-created the brand Get Lean Gluten Free; where he continually develops healthy eating nutritional books and programs.

Jeremy's blog has been named top 20 fitness blogs by Breaking Muscle in 2013 & 2014. SHAPE Magazine named him one of the 50 Hottest Trainers in America in 2013 & 2014. He has been featured on numerous sites and publications such as Muscle & Fitness, Bodybuilding.com, Livestrong.com and Simply Gluten Free Magazine among others. Jeremy is currently a PROLAB/MRI and Reebok sponsored athlete.

He's a fitness junkie at heart whose passion for his client's success can only be outmatched by his work ethic for it. Jeremy prides himself on giving you authentic, unfiltered, no bullshit truth about health, fitness, and real life advice to help you make success mandatory in your life.

Opportunities to connect personally with Jeremy and his team:

Visit our website at: www.jeremyscottfitness.com

Email us at: jeremyscottfitness@hotmail.com

We look forward to working with and hearing all about your future success.

Manufactured by Amazon.ca
Bolton, ON

10807089R00042